SandCastle™

First Rhymes

Dunk-Tank Frank

Anders Hanson

Consulting Editor, Diane Craig, M.A./Reading Specialist

ABDO
Publishing Company

Published by ABDO Publishing Company, 4940 Viking Drive, Edina, Minnesota 55435.

Printed in the United States.

Credits
Edited by: Pam Price
Curriculum Coordinator: Nancy Tuminelly
Cover and Interior Design and Production: Mighty Media
Photo Credits: AbleStock, Corbis Images, Anders Hanson, Photodisc

Library of Congress Cataloging-in-Publication Data

Hanson, Anders, 1980-
    Dunk-tank Frank / Anders Hanson.
       p. cm. -- (First rhymes)
    ISBN 1-59679-475-5 (hardcover)
    ISBN 1-59679-476-3 (paperback)
       1. English language--Rhyme--Juvenile literature. I. Title. II. Series.
    PE1517.H365 2005
    808.1--dc22

                                                                        2005048027

SandCastle™ books are created by a professional team of educators, reading specialists, and content developers around five essential components that include phonemic awareness, phonics, vocabulary, text comprehension, and fluency. All books are written, reviewed, and leveled for guided reading and early intervention reading, and designed for use in shared, guided, and independent reading and writing activities to support a balanced approach to literacy instruction.

Let Us Know

After reading the book, SandCastle would like you to tell us your stories about reading. What is your favorite page? Was there something hard that you needed help with? Share the ups and downs of learning to read. We want to hear from you! To get posted on the ABDO Publishing Company Web site, send us e-mail at:

sandcastle@abdopub.com

SandCastle Level: Beginning

3 1561 00181 7992

-ank

bank

crank

plank

sank

tank

Look at the  .

Here is the  .

This is the .

The boat .

Look at the  .

The bank is brown.

The crank can turn.

The plank is long.

The boat sank
in the water.

The tank has fish.

Dunk-Tank Frank

Frank is on
a long plank.

The plank
is over a tank.

Put in a BUCK
Give me a YANK

There is a crank
on the tank
under the plank.

A sign says,
"Put in a buck.
Give me a yank!"

Hank went to the bank
to get a buck to yank
the crank on the tank
with the plank.

Hank put in the buck
from the bank
and gave the crank
a yank.

Away went the plank,
and poor Frank
sank in the tank!

About SandCastle™

A professional team of educators, reading specialists, and content developers created the SandCastle™ series to support young readers as they develop reading skills and strategies and increase their general knowledge. The SandCastle™ series has four levels that correspond to early literacy development in young children. The levels are provided to help teachers and parents select the appropriate books for young readers.

Emerging Readers
(no flags)

Beginning Readers
(1 flag)

Transitional Readers
(2 flags)

Fluent Readers
(3 flags)

These levels are meant only as a guide. All levels are subject to change.

To see a complete list of SandCastle™ books and other nonfiction titles from ABDO Publishing Company, visit www.abdopub.com or contact us at:
4940 Viking Drive, Edina, Minnesota 55435 • 1-800-800-1312 • fax: 1-952-831-1632